This is Kazoo

This book is dedicated to all
the wonderful people who encouraged
me to create this book.

Kazoo is half Irish Wolfhound/Great Pyrenees mix.

He is two years old and currently lives in Campbell River, BC.

Kazoo is spunky, stubborn, energetic, and full of love.

"Hi! I'm Kazoo. Let me tell you about some of the things I like to do and little bit about my life."

"Every morning I like to say "HI" to my neighbors. I like to be really loud so they hear me, even if they are sleeping. I'm kind of like an unexpected alarm clock."

"Chewing bones is my favorite. I also like chewing sticks, teddy bears, balls, socks, cardboard...."

"This is my crate. I sleep in here. Sometimes I have to take a break in here when I need to calm down but shhh.. I'm really good at escaping."

"I enjoy all kinds of adventures. Mountains are my absolute favorite. I like to run all the way to the top, take a little nap, and run all the way back down."

"In order to go on adventures, I need to ride in the car. Good thing I like the car. I put my head out the window and let the wind blow through my hair or just take a nap."

"This is me in the bathtub. I don't actually like baths but I do love water. I'm really messy in the bath, I like to cover the whole bathroom in water and after I run away."

"Cuddling is my favorite. I like to snuggle my pillow at night and put my blanket on. I fall asleep and dream about all the fun things I'll do tomorrow."

The End

Next up in the series: This is Duke

Next up in the series: This is Ru

Manufactured by Amazon.ca
Bolton, ON

24500719R00017